Dedicated to those who feel battered and shipwrecked —with only
a dream to keep them afloat.

Butterfly Tree Press
ISBN: 978-0-9960615-7-5

Copyright 2020
All paintings by Donna Drejza.

Not to be copied or reproduced without permission.

Flute Dancer

# What is a Renaissance Person?

A Renaissance person has knowledge and proficiency in many fields.

Renaissance people are intelligent and active people with a thirst for knowledge and a desire to live out loud and in color.

The Renaissance person is not your ordinary person. They use all of their senses, even their sixth sense. Renaissance people are travelers. The best way to learn about architecture, art, cuisine, languages, culture and people — is through travel.

Renaissance people are interested and therefore interesting. They are fearless, thoughtful and most of all kind.

If you wish to become a Renaissance person, you may start as a grasshopper and work your way up to a master. This doesn't happen overnight, and it is a life-long process. There is no ending to learning, just a beginning. The goal of this book is to inspire. Are you ready to Renaissance Now?

Efrem Zimbalist, Sr. and Alma Gluck

## A Little History:

The Renaissance, was believed to have begun in the 14$^{th}$ century in Italy, and spread to the rest of Europe over the next few centuries. But who can remember. After the middle ages, it was a time of cultural, artistic, political and scientific rebirth.

**Leonardo da Vinci -** 1452-1519  Italy. He was the primo Renaissance man who, among other things, was a painter, mathematician, engineer, architect, botanist, sculptor and anatomist. In his free time, he painted the Mona Lisa.

**Michelangelo -**  1475-1564  Italy. He was a sculptor, painter, architect, poet and engineer. Known for the Statue of David and St. Peter's Basilica.

**Nicolas Copernicus -**  1473-1543  Poland. He was a master of astronomy, medicine, governance and economics. Known for his heliocentric model of the planets and his "Theory of Money," in Economics.

# The Top Ten:

Here are the top ten men of The Renaissance, and a great place to start reading biographies.

- Leonardo da Vinci.
- William Shakespeare.
- Nicolaus Copernicus.
- Michelangelo.
- Galileo Galilei.
- Raphael.
- Michel de Montaigne.
- Filippo Brunelleschi.
- Petrarch.
- Lorenzo de' Medici.

Asian Princess

# Renaissance Women:

One could write a book on the unsung sparrows of all time. This list will evolve, but is a good start for your research.

- Sofonisba Anguissola
- Bianca Maria Visconti
- Catherine de Medici
- Isabella d'Este Musée du Louvre
- Marguerite D'Angoulême
- Queen Isabella of Aragon
- Lucrezia Borgia
- Marie Curie
- Beatrix Potter
- Jane Goodall
- Hedy Lamarr
- Eileen Gray
- Condoleezza Rice

Charles, Prince of Wales

# Charles, Prince of Wales:

A modern day Renaissance man, Prince Charles is one of my favorites —and not just because I have a painting of him. In my book, Charles is a five-star Renaissance man.

In addition to being the Prince of Wales, Charles is a patron of 350 charitable organizations, an author, environmentalist, historical preservationist, painter, organic farmer, world traveler, pianist and cellist, and speaker of French, German, Welsh and Gaelic. It is likely that I have missed a few of his interests.

James Bond House Lake Como

# Finding Inspiration:

These are my modern day semi- fictitious Renaissance characters. Why not start by writing your own dream biography?

Gene: father, lawyer, plays clarinet, bakes cakes, bird watcher, who speaks German.

Lola: fashion designer, speaks Italian, is an oenophile, and paints landscapes.

Jack: architect, watercolorist, photographer, gourmet cook and expert on scotch.

Mary: traveler, speaks French and Italian, restores and sails old boats, studies butterflies.

Simon: traveler, architect, yachtsman, farmer, writer, speaker of French.

Angela: traveler, journalist, novelist, who speaks Mandarin.

John: traveler, engineer, boater, inventor, trumpet player, golfer.

Queen Watching a Parade

# Foreign Travel:

- Renaissance people are travelers. They are fascinated with places different from their own. The history, the architecture, the language, the cuisine, the culture of foreign lands fascinates them.

- Traveling takes time and money, and one rarely has both at the same time. If you let this be an obstacle, you'll never go anywhere. One can travel on a dime, and one can travel in little time. If you have no one with travel with, relish this freedom. There is nothing worse than a poor travel mate. (That is unless you are plotting a murder mystery.)

- If you are locked down with no possible way to travel, then take a journey in your mind. Pretend you are going to Italy for 2 weeks, even if you never leave the house. Look up flights, hotels, restaurants, museums, and sights from your armchair.

- Half of the experience is in the planning and the anticipation. If you can't go, then use online or roll up maps and walk through the streets virtually. Look up the menus of fine restaurants, and cook the food and drink the wine from home.

Ceremony by the Sea (Asian boy)

# Foreign Language:

- A Renaissance person can speak at least one foreign language. If you are not blessed with this gift, you'll just have to try, try again.

- Choose a language that excites you. French, German, Italian, Russian, Hindi, Mandarin, Swahili. Your choice. The more exotic the better.

- Find your way of learning. Try classes, online learning, books, or carry around a little dictionary. (I have to write everything 10 times, and color code.)

- Immerse yourself by thinking in that language, watching movies, and making friends who speak that language.

- Visit the country. Be daring and get a one-way ticket and stay.

- If you can't decide on a language, then choose three. Start with the basics, like how to order a glass of wine. Or better yet, a bottle so you don't have to order again.

A Room with a View

# Music:

- A true Renaissance person can play at least one musical instrument. What have you always longed to play? The piano, flute, clarinet, harp, saxophone, or the drums?

- Try writing a song. Maybe a haunting melody on a piano by using some of the black keys.

- Write some heartfelt lyrics by starting with a poem and repeating with refrains, bridges and a chorus.

- Buy an old 78 record player and some old records by Benny Goodman or Lawrence Tibbett.

- Play an opera aria, make spaghetti sauce, and imagine your next encounter. Evoke your sense of taste, smell, feel, sight, sound — and intuition.

- Listen and discover your favorite composers. Debussy, Mozart, Chopin made magic.

- Visit jazz clubs and jazz festivals. Get some Dave Brubeck and Miles Davis albums.

Robert Palmer

# Style:

- A Renaissance person develops their own sense of style, and is never a lemming or fashion victim.

- Become vintage by watching old movies or shows like The Thin Man. Look through books, and then visit vintage shops.

- Take time to develop a wardrobe. One for work, one for travel — and one for drinking absinthe.

- Do not wear sports clothes if you are not actually playing a sport.

- Be the one who brings back the Marabou Peignoir and the velvet smoking jacket.

- Wear ascots, capes, evening gowns, and boots — and you will instantly feel more adventurous. But not all at once.

- Wear a hat. You won't have to worry about your hair and you'll look jaunty.

- Buy fine old Italian goods like handbags, shoes, luggage and a fountain pen.

Downton Abbey Dance

# Activities:

- A Renaissance person has no time to watch someone else playing a sport.

- Take up fencing — the terms are in French and the outfit is flattering.

- Choose two or three new sports or activities to take up: chess, darts, archery, hiking, rafting, polo, tennis, golf, fishing.

- Dance. Observe the various dance movements. Choose one and master it, like the Viennese Waltz.

- Ballet. Go to the ballet and drink in the beauty. It is okay to be a spectator of ballet.

Sunday in Lucerne

# Design:

- Visit used book stores for coffee table books on architecture and design.

- Learn the various styles of architecture, and decide on your favorites.

- Get some drafting paper and design your dream house with a floor plan and elevation.

- Pretend you have $12m to spend on 4 dream houses around the world.

- Look on sites and books for inspiration. Design a living room from the 1880's Paris or 1920's London.

Malta Jazz 1949

# Dramatic Arts:

- Become an expert on one country, like Denmark and watch all of the films in Danish with subtitles.

- Watch classic black & white films like Night of the Iguana, Casablanca and Schindler's List.

- Study the plays of Oscar Wilde, Arthur Miller, Henrik Ibsen and Tennessee Williams. Now, write your own torrid masterpiece.

- Have a contest with yourself and come up with your favorite 100 movies of all time.

- Experience The Vienna Philharmonic, Teatro alla Scalla in Milan, The Moulin Rouge in Paris, and a concert at The Royal Albert Hall in London. Or pretend.

54

Empire Sofa and Imaginary Cats

# Collecting:

- Alas, a Renaissance person always chooses form over function. A tiny Empire setae — never an Ikea leather sofa.

- Study antiques and learn the periods and styles of: Victorian, Gothic, Rococo, and Empire.

- Learn the differences between artifacts of the Tang, Sung, Ming and Qing Dynasties.

- Study the French Impressionists, such as Monet, Renoir, Cezanne, and Vuillard. Find your favorites.

- Learn the famous Abstract artists of the 20$^{th}$ century.

- Visit in person or online: The British Museum, The Louvre, The Natural History Museum, Galleria degli Uffizi, Vatican Museums, State Hermitage Museum, The National Palace Museum, and The National Archaeological Museum.

John F. Kennedy

# History:

- A Renaissance person can spin an antique globe and be able to identify the former countries.

- Study the boundaries of countries and how they have changed.

- Read a book on European history.

- Understand the impetus for such major events as Russian revolution, the WWI, WWII.

- Read biographies of famous people like Napoleon, Winston Churchill and John F. Kennedy.

- Watch historical movies and documentaries.

- Select one country and become a historical expert.

- Go to your ancestral town and read all of the plaques, and landmarks. Discover why your ancestors left.

Hugh Grant in Sense and Sensibility

# Literature:

- Find and read the 100 best books of all time. Ideas: Madam Bovary, 1984, Anna Karenina, Love in a Time of Cholera.

- Write a short story about your life. Live your life so it will make a great story. I'm writing, "Adventures in a Time of Corona."

- Buy some old poetry books, and sit in a garden and read them aloud.

- Write a poem in a foreign language to a fictional lover. French would be pretty.

- Write seven heartfelt poems to someone you love —or your dog.

- Write a novel. Yes, you can.

Asian Houses – pink and green

# Arts:

- Learn the color wheel and the differences between contrasting and complimentary colors.

- Become an oil or water color painter by buying a kit and starting with a still life of a pear or the sea.

- Get an old camera and take black and white photos pretending it's London in 1940.

- Make a dark room out of a bathroom, and learn to develop your own film.

- Take color photos of insects and rain drops on plants.

Richmond, UK Boats

## Nautical/Aeronautical:

- A Renaissance person would never be seen on a new vessel, instead preferring an antique or classic boat, such as a Chris Craft or Garwood.

- Go for a sail on an old sea trawler or cargo ship.

- Take a boating or sailing class. Better yet, become a yacht captain. (10 points!)

- Read Yacht Design magazines and design a mega yacht.

- Learn all of the parts of a boat and boating terminology.

- Life is short: if you are still interested, then buy and old boat. (Blame the aftermath on me.)

- Study the dynamics of aeronautical design.

- Become a pilot (20 points)

Pink Cake

# Cuisine:

- Read cookbooks by famous chefs such as Julia Childs, Jacques Pepin, Daniel Boulud, Alain Ducasse.

- Choose one country and learn to make the specialties. Ideas: French, Italian, Spanish, Indian.

- Become an amateur French chef. Learn to make Pate, Duck a' Orange, and French sauces.

- Master an elegant dessert such as Zabaglione, Gran Marnier soufflé, or Linzer torte.

- Learn Morisuke, the Japanese art of food arranging.

- Become a chocolatier in your own home. Buy bulk chocolates, molds, and pretty boxes and ribbons.

- Dream by studying the menus of 5 star and Michelin star restaurants around the world. Make a plan to visit them in real life.

Eggplant and Sancerre

# Wine/Spirits:

- A Renaissance person will chose quality over quantity by saving up for a fine bottle of Chateau Palmer Margaux, in lieu of large amounts of inferior wines.

- Become an oenophile, by reading up on wines and having your own wine tastings.

- Learn all of the wine regions of France and Italy and then make a plan to travel to the regions one by one.

- Learn all of the varieties of grapes and learn to distinguish between them.

- Train to be a sommelier (20 points).

- Learn the subtleties of single malt scotch. Be able to tell the difference between a Highland, Lowland, Islay and Speyside. Or have fun trying.

Sea Society

# Animals/Wildlife:

- A Renaissance person spends time in a quiet garden with a noisy dog.

- Pretend you are running the Westminster Dog Show, and learn to identify all of the dog breeds. But adopt a mutt from the pound.

- Cats (some) make great pets. Fish are lovely and usually quiet.

- Get some binoculars and become a birdwatcher.

- Become a closet Lepidopterist by studying butterflies.

- Get some colored pencils and design a dream garden.

- Look up all of the famous gardens of England and France. Take an older relative to visit them someday.

- When the time is right, create your own garden. Learn the various trees, shrubs, plants and flowers that will make you happy and serene.

Colored Particles

## Math/Science:

- A Renaissance person is fascinated by math and science. They often own a microscope, binoculars, a telescope and a slide rule.

- Engineers, doctors and scientists are lovely and fascinating people. If you are not one, try to befriend one.

- Learn all of the elements on the periodic chart. You just might end up inheriting a Rhodium mine.

- Invent something! Maybe something that uses mechanical or electrical power, or magnets.

- Learn the importance of mathematics in one single instance. Try to calculate the volume of an airplane luggage hold.

- Learn all of the planets in relationship to one another by making a mobile in the style of Calder.

Three Dancers - Orange and Blue

# Mindfulness:

- A Renaissance person strives to be kind, caring and soulful. This takes practice — and the avoidance of annoying people.

- Start the day by thinking of others. Or just one other person. What can you do to make their day?

- Practice being mindful of each word you say. Is it kind, necessary and truthful?

- Think of every word and action that drives you. Is it based on ego? If so, rethink it.

- Try to do good deeds secretly.

- Learn to be quiet. Do not pollute the lovely silence of a moment with an unprocessed data dump. Aim to be a monk, not a jabberwocky.

- Slow down and appreciate the moment. It will never come back.

- Write in a journal. It's easier to collect your thoughts on paper.

Bride and Groom -pink

# Religion/Spiritual:

- A Renaissance person seeks to understand others.

- Try to get an overview of 7 different religions.

- Pick one and study that religion and practice it for a year. Choose a new religion every year.

- Visit a mosque, a church, a synagogue, and a temple.

- Find a way to observe and appreciate a Jewish, Greek, Indian, Chinese and an Italian wedding.

- Practice observing the holidays of each religion.

- Be open minded enough to believe in the possibility of gods, angels, reincarnation, and past lives.

Little Houses on the Hill

I hope you are inspired, because it's time for another world-wide renaissance.

With love, Donna

Butterfly Tree Press
ISBN: 978-0-9960615-7-5

Copyright 2020
All paintings by Donna Drejza
Not to be copied or reproduced without permission.

For more information on the paintings and other books, visit:

DonnaDrejza.com

www.ingramcontent.com/pod-product-compliance
Lightning Source LLC
Chambersburg PA
CBHW040059160426
43193CB00002B/22